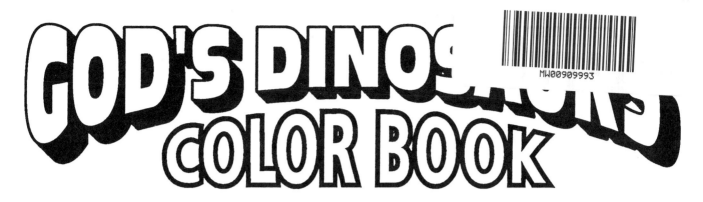

GOD'S DINOSAURS COLOR BOOK

AN ACTIVITY BOOK ALL ABOUT COLORS
Written and Illustrated by Earl and Bonita Snellenberger

You are worthy, O Lord, to receive glory and honor and power; For You created all things, And by Your will they exist and were created. *Revelation 4:11*

Praise God who created many kinds of dinosaurs.

What colors did He make them? No one knows.

Let's use our imaginations with the dinosaurs in this book,

And make each a different color from its head down to its toes.

Note to parents and teachers: You may want to assure proper color identification by helping young children find the correct color to fill in the crayon at the top of each page.

ISBN 0-89051-171-3

color blue

God made the light blue sky above
A bright Blue Jay in a tree. . .

You can make different kinds of blue (light blue or dark blue)
by pressing lighter or harder with the same crayon. Or you may have
different kinds of blue if you have a large box of crayons.

Blue Jay

The Blue Jay's crest, back, wings, and tail are **blue**. Its face and breast are white.

color  blue

And a blue Anchisaurus eating big blueberries
On the shore of a deep blue sea.

And worship Him that made heaven, and earth, and the sea. . .
Revelation 14:7

ANCHISAURUS
(AN-ki-SORE-us)

Name means "close reptile"
Plant and meat-eater
8 feet long

Connect the dots to
spell **blue** to finish
the Anchisaurus' tail.

color **yellow**

EDMONTOSAURUS
(ed-MON-toh-SORE-us)

Name means "Edmonton reptile"
(Named for a rock formation)
Plant-eater
43 feet long

You (God) have prepared
the light and the sun.
Psalm 74:16

Trace over the
dotted line to finish
drawing the pear.

God's yellow sun shines over the hill
On yellow baby ducks playing hide and seek.
Sweet yellow pears are a tasty meal
For a yellow dinosaur with a duck-like beak.

color [yellow]

A yellow canary in a yellow banana tree
   Sings a song so sweet and free,
As a yellow Saurolophus stops to eat a bunch for lunch
   And goes his way merrily.

Finish the canary's body by connecting the dots to spell **yellow**.

SAUROLOPHUS
(SORE-oh-LOAF-us)

Name means "ridged reptile"
Plant-eater
30 feet long

color red

Red roses, red poppies, and bright red cherries—
God created many red things, beautiful and sweet.

And the earth brought forth grass, the herb that yields seed according to its kind, and the tree that yields fruit, whose seed is in itself according to its kind. And God saw that it was good. *Genesis 1:12*

Lady

color red

God made red apples, red tomatoes, and red strawberries,
Good things for a big red dinosaur to eat.

Cardinal **e**
          •
          •

r •   **d**
    •   •

Finish the Cardinal's head crest
by connecting the dots to spell **red**.

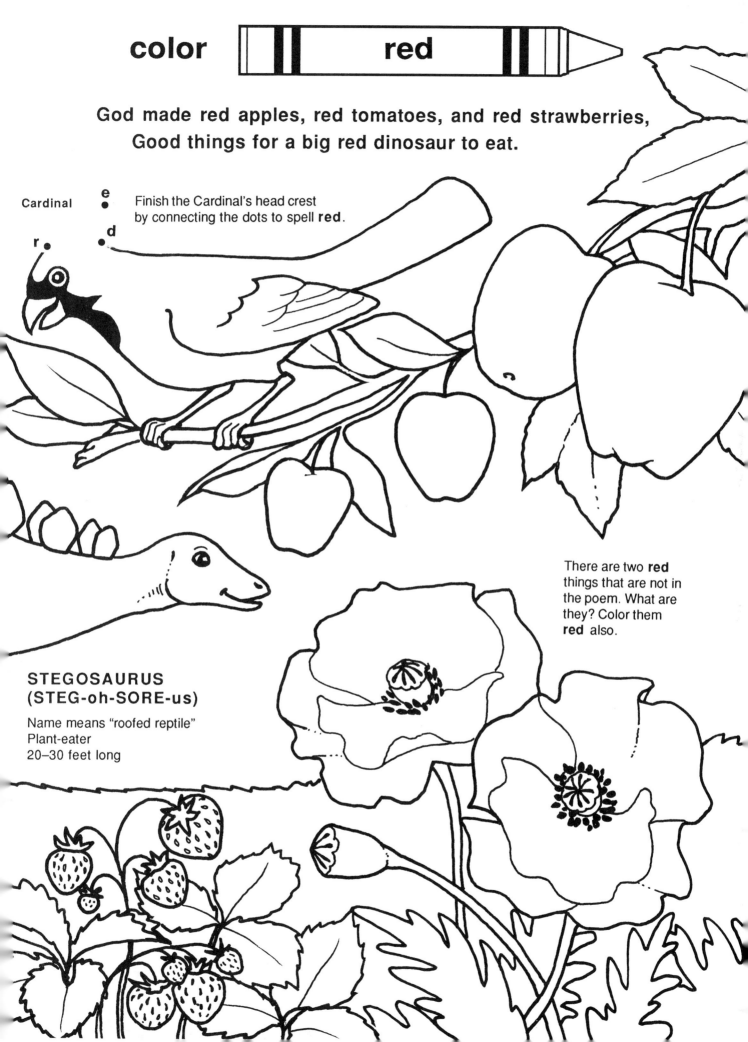

There are two **red**
things that are not in
the poem. What are
they? Color them
red also.

STEGOSAURUS
(STEG-oh-SORE-us)

Name means "roofed reptile"
Plant-eater
20–30 feet long

color **orange**

**CERATOSAURUS
(SAIR-ah-toe-SORE-us**

Name means "horned reptile"
Meat-eater
20 feet long

Color the dinosaur
orange. Then draw
more black spots on
its body.

**Round juicy oranges growing on a tree,
Orange pumpkins and orange gourds,
The striped orange tiger and the spotted orange dinosaur—
All of them are the Lord's.**

God...made the world and everything in it... *Acts 17:24*

color

purple

The color PURPLE is also known as VIOLET.

PACHYCEPHALOSAURUS
(PACK-ee-CEF-ah-loh-SORE-us)

Name means "thick-headed lizard"
Plant-eater
15 feet long
Some scientists believe that male dinosaurs
of this kind charged each other and butted
heads as do male sheep and goats.

Butting their thick-skulled heads together,
  Two purple dinosaurs run around.
Purple plums and grapes grow above them,
  Purple violets cover the ground.

color green

Finish the Triceratop's back by connecting the dots to spell **green**.

TRICERATOPS
(tri-SAIR-ah-tops)

Name means "three-horned face"
Plant-eater
30 feet long

A green frog on a green lilly pad gives three mighty hops
Over a slow green turtle to land on a green Triceratops.

color green

PSITTACOSAURUS
(sie-TACK-oh-SORE-us)

Name means "parrot lizard"
Plant-eater
6 feet long

Also, to every beast of the earth, to every
bird of the air, and to everything that creeps
on the earth, in which there is life, I (God) have
given every green herb for food ; and it was so.
Genesis 1:30

A green parrot in a green-leafed tree
    Is eating green grapes for a treat
While a green Psittacosaurus is having
    Green beans and green cabbage to eat.

color brown

SPINOSAURUS
(SPINE-oh-SORE-us)

Name means "spiny reptile"
Meat-eater
40 feet long

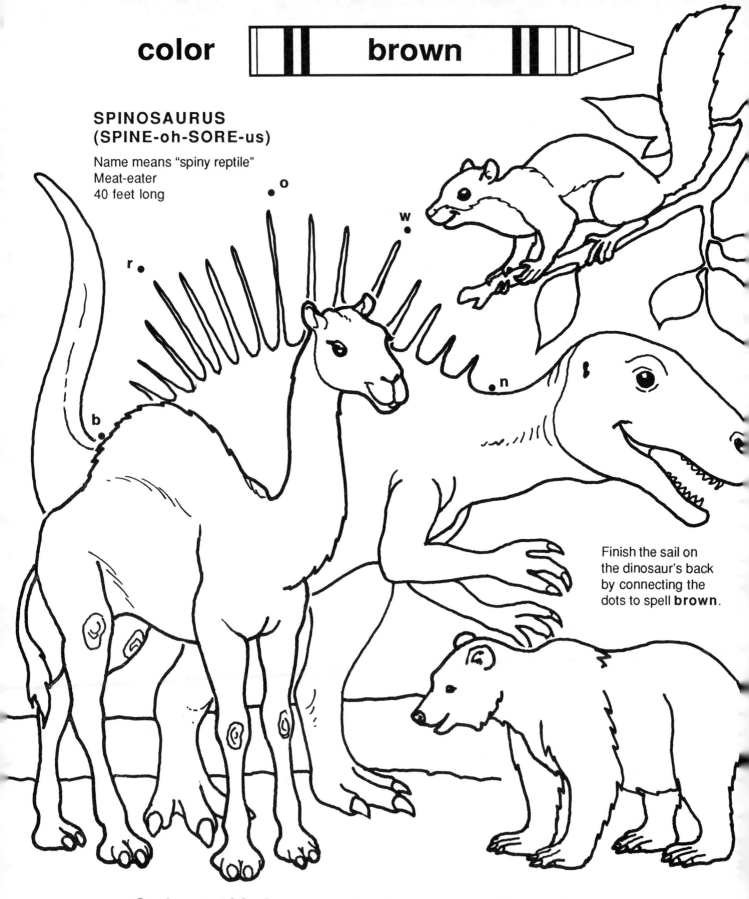

Finish the sail on
the dinosaur's back
by connecting the
dots to spell **brown**.

God put a big hump on the brown camel's back.
To the brown Spinosaurus He gave a big sail.
God made the brown bear with big paws and long claws.
To the brown squirrel God gave a big, fluffy tail.

color pink

If you do not have a pink crayon, press lightly
with a red crayon to make pink.

God made the pink flamingo that wades in the water
With brightly colored feathers as clean as can be.
And God also made the pink pig and the pink Eryops
That wallow in the dirty mud and grunt so happily.

Trace over the dotted
line to give Eryops a
strong back and tail.

ERYOPS
(ER-ee-ops)

Name means "drawn-out face"
Meat-eater
7 feet long
Not truly a dinosaur, but an amphibian that lived
in and near streams and ponds.

color ▰▰ black ▰▰ ·······

A black and white Tyrannosaurus is surprised to see
A furry panda, white and black, eating bamboo at his knee.

Color the areas of animals
marked with a dotted B **black**.
Leave other areas **white**.

TYRANNOSAURUS
(tie-RAN-oh-SORE-us)

Name means "tyrant lizard"
Meat-eater
50 feet long

Above Tyrannosaurus flies a blackbird and a black bat.
And on the dinosaur's broad back there climbs a slinky black cat.

·····and ····· **white**

An ostrich with feathers of white and of black
Chases a dinosaur with spots on its back.

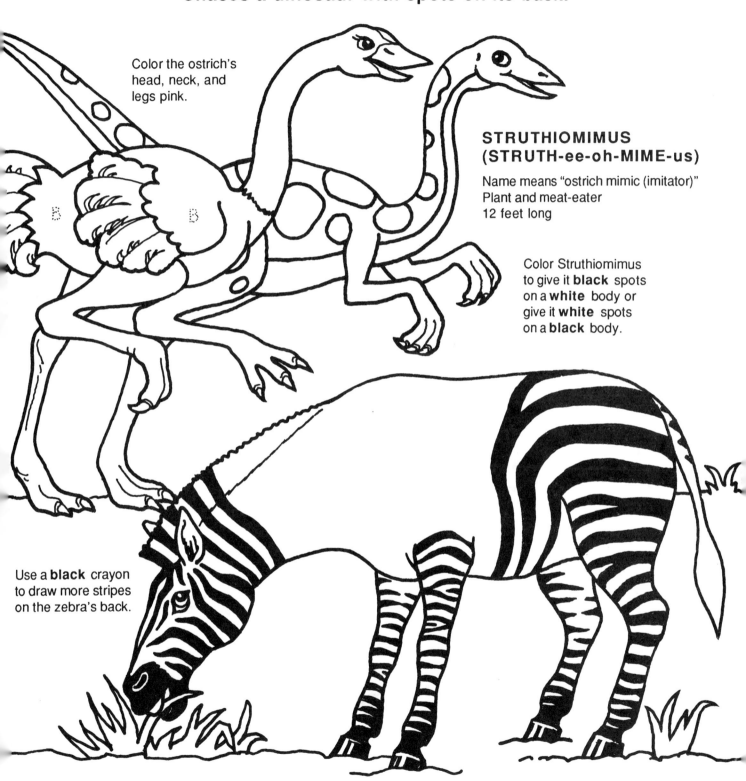

Color the ostrich's head, neck, and legs pink.

**STRUTHIOMIMUS
(STRUTH-ee-oh-MIME-us)**

Name means "ostrich mimic (imitator)"
Plant and meat-eater
12 feet long

Color Struthiomimus to give it **black** spots on a **white** body or give it **white** spots on a **black** body.

Use a **black** crayon to draw more stripes on the zebra's back.

But the black and white zebra has no time to play.
It just wants to eat tasty grass all the day.

MATCHING DINOSAURS

God made a male and female of each kind of animal He created (Genesis 1). Draw a line from each dinosaur on the left to its matching mate on the right. Make matching dinosaurs the same color.

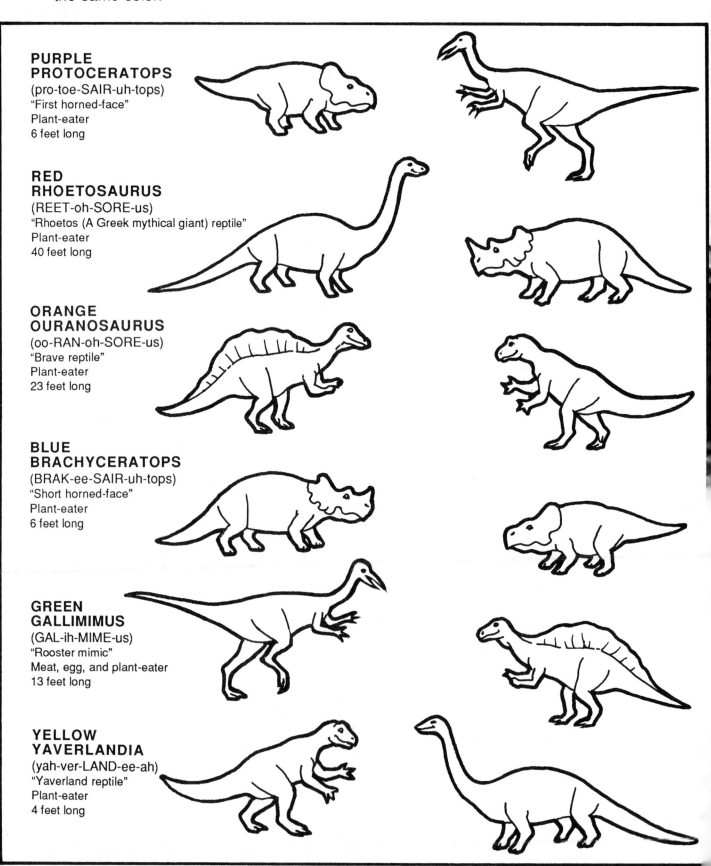

PURPLE PROTOCERATOPS
(pro-toe-SAIR-uh-tops)
"First horned-face"
Plant-eater
6 feet long

RED RHOETOSAURUS
(REET-oh-SORE-us)
"Rhoetos (A Greek mythical giant) reptile"
Plant-eater
40 feet long

ORANGE OURANOSAURUS
(oo-RAN-oh-SORE-us)
"Brave reptile"
Plant-eater
23 feet long

BLUE BRACHYCERATOPS
(BRAK-ee-SAIR-uh-tops)
"Short horned-face"
Plant-eater
6 feet long

GREEN GALLIMIMUS
(GAL-ih-MIME-us)
"Rooster mimic"
Meat, egg, and plant-eater
13 feet long

YELLOW YAVERLANDIA
(yah-ver-LAND-ee-ah)
"Yaverland reptile"
Plant-eater
4 feet long